3 0132 02141772 5

D0532706

I Love
Animal
Homes

Northumberland Schools Library Service	
3 0132 02141772 5	
Askews & Holts	Dec-2012
S591 GREEN	£5.99

By Lisa Regan
Illustrated by Ian Jackson

MiLes KeLLy

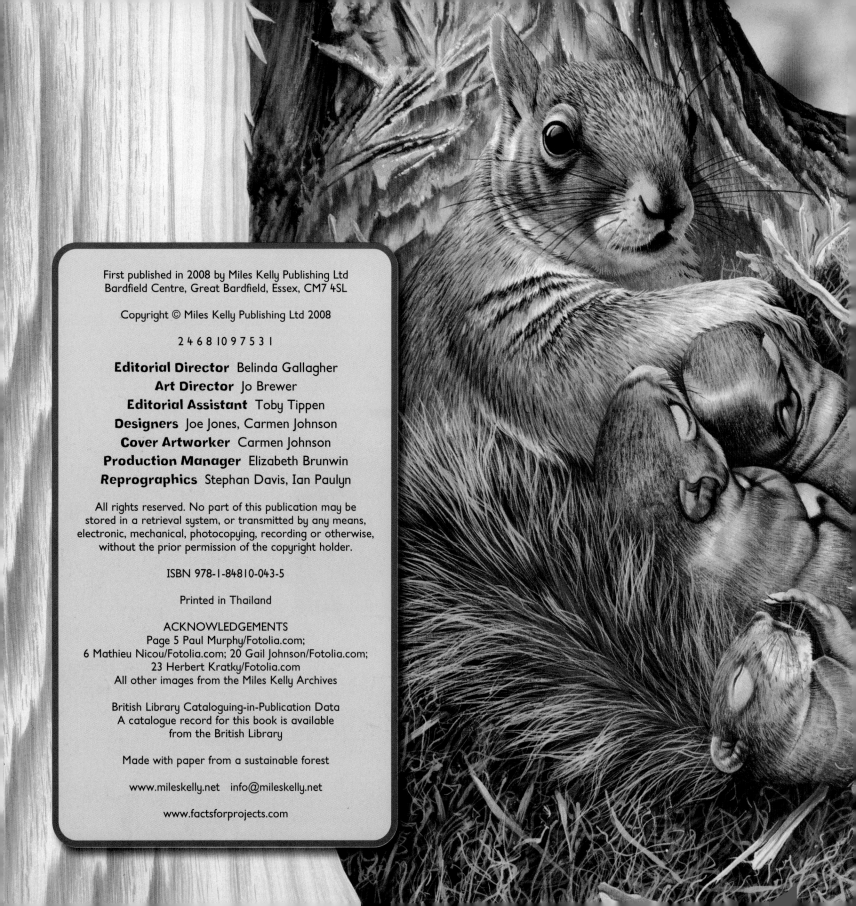

First published in 2008 by Miles Kelly Publishing Ltd
Bardfield Centre, Great Bardfield, Essex, CM7 4SL

Copyright © Miles Kelly Publishing Ltd 2008

2 4 6 8 10 9 7 5 3 1

Editorial Director Belinda Gallagher
Art Director Jo Brewer
Editorial Assistant Toby Tippen
Designers Joe Jones, Carmen Johnson
Cover Artworker Carmen Johnson
Production Manager Elizabeth Brunwin
Reprographics Stephan Davis, Ian Paulyn

All rights reserved. No part of this publication may be
stored in a retrieval system, or transmitted by any means,
electronic, mechanical, photocopying, recording or otherwise,
without the prior permission of the copyright holder.

ISBN 978-1-84810-043-5

Printed in Thailand

ACKNOWLEDGEMENTS
Page 5 Paul Murphy/Fotolia.com;
6 Mathieu Nicou/Fotolia.com; 20 Gail Johnson/Fotolia.com;
23 Herbert Kratky/Fotolia.com
All other images from the Miles Kelly Archives

British Library Cataloguing-in-Publication Data
A catalogue record for this book is available
from the British Library

Made with paper from a sustainable forest

www.mileskelly.net   info@mileskelly.net

www.factsforprojects.com

Contents

Dormouse nest

A dormouse nest looks like a ball of twigs.
Dormice build their nests in hedges or underneath trees. The nests are actually made of grass, leaves and tree bark, torn into little pieces. The dormouse curls up in its cosy home to sleep all winter. This is called hibernation.

An adult dormouse is tiny. When it curls up to sleep, it is only about as big as your fist.

Dormice can hibernate for half of the year! Their bodies grow cold and they look like they are hardly breathing.

In autumn, a dormouse's main food is nuts. Dormice eat lots to fatten themselves up, ready for hibernation.

Making sense
Mice have poor eyesight, so they use their whiskers to sense air movement to help them avoid predators.

Dormice usually have four babies. The young are born in the summer and autumn when there is lots of food to eat.

5

Beaver lodge

Beavers live near rivers and streams. They build a home of sticks, grass and mud, which is called a lodge. Beavers have big, sharp teeth that they use to chew through trees. The beavers use the wood to build a dam across the water, which stops the lodge from being washed away.

During winter, piles of sticks are stored in the water so that beavers can nibble at the bark. In spring they eat buds and shoots.

Special fur

Oily, waterproof fur keeps beavers' skin dry and enables them to stay warm in cold water.

The entrance to the lodge is an underwater tunnel. This stops other animals from getting inside.

Ant colony

Millions of ants live in a home called a colony. The ants build the colony and keep it safe and clean. They carry bits of dirt to the colony, which build up into a small hill above ground. Underground, there are holes, or chambers. Here, the ants store food and raise their young.

The queen's job is to lay eggs. Other female ants keep the eggs clean and bring food for the queen.

Ants with wings are either queens or males. The queens are much bigger than the males.

Super home
Termites are insects that build and live in mounds that can reach 9 metres high. That's about five times taller than an adult man.

The white eggs turn into larvae. These are young ants and they need lots of food to grow.

The larvae become covered in silky thread called a cocoon. Soon, grown-up ants will break out of the cocoons.

Polar bear den

When she is ready to have her babies, a female polar bear digs a den in the snow. Her cubs are born in winter so the den keeps them safe and warm. Mother and cubs remain in the den until the spring. Then, the cubs are big enough to leave their home.

When they are first born, the cubs are blind and helpless. They grow very quickly.

Most dens are made in snowdrifts. The mother digs deep into the snow with her strong paws and claws.

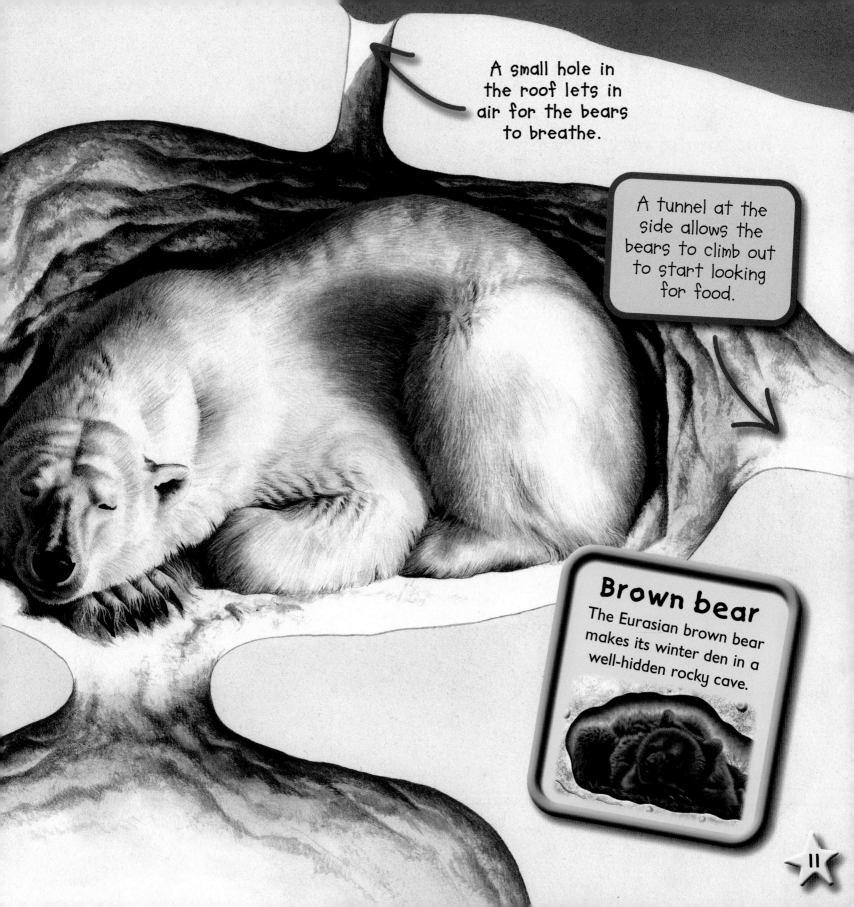

A small hole in the roof lets in air for the bears to breathe.

A tunnel at the side allows the bears to climb out to start looking for food.

Brown bear

The Eurasian brown bear makes its winter den in a well-hidden rocky cave.

Fox den

A fox family may have more than one den, or home. Before a female fox, or vixen, has her babies, she makes several dens. These can be under tree trunks or in old rabbit holes. When the cubs, are born, their mother may move them to a new den if the old one is disturbed.

The mother fox may have up to six cubs. They don't open their eyes until they are nearly two weeks old.

Foxes may dig their own dens, but they prefer to find an old rabbit hole and make it bigger.

The cubs venture outside their den when they are one month old. They like to play with each other.

Snow home
Arctic foxes make snow dens that can be more than 3 metres underground!

Weaver bird nest

These birds get their name from the way they weave their nests like baskets. Lots of weaver birds build their nests close together in the branches of the same tree. The male bird builds the nest. He shows it off to the females to encourage them to choose him as a mate.

Neat nest

Birds nests can be different shapes and sizes. These Cape Batis birds have built a small, neat nest.

The male bird hangs outside the nest and uses his beak to wind strands of grass in and out.

The female lays her eggs in the main hollow. She sits on the eggs to keep them warm until they hatch.

The nests are fastened tightly to the tree. Once the male has found a mate, he completes the entrance tunnel.

The entrance tunnel is the only way into the nest. It stops predators such as snakes stealing the eggs and chicks.

Wasp nest

Thousands of wasps live in one nest.
The nest is built with a papery substance
that the wasps make. The paper is used
to create small cells. Here, the queen
wasp lays her eggs. Worker wasps
hatch from the eggs and help
to make the nest bigger.

The wasps make
paper by chewing
wood and mixing
it with their spit.

A queen sleeps
through the winter,
ready to start a new
nest in the spring.
The rest of the wasps
die in the cold.

Be careful!
Wasps have a painful sting on their rear ends. They may use it on any creature that disturbs their nest.

The workers add paper around the outside of the cells. This helps to protect the whole nest.

Look out for wasps' nests in roofs, garden sheds, hollow trees and holes in the ground.

Hermit crab shell

As they don't have their own shells, hermit crabs have to find one! These creatures have soft bodies that are easy for predators to eat. To stay safe, the crabs hide inside empty seashells. They poke their legs and head outside the shell so they can move and find food.

As the crab grows bigger, it leaves its old shell to look for a new one with more room.

Under cover
Once it has crawled into a shell, a hermit crab carries its home on its back.

Most hermit crabs choose snail shells to live in. The shell needs to be in one piece, with no holes in.

This hairy yellow hermit crab lives on coral reefs, where it picks up food with its claws.

Once it has found a shell, the hermit crab climbs into it backwards. This means it can keep a lookout for danger.

Squirrel nest

Squirrels make nests high up in the treetops.
The nests are good homes for baby squirrels, and
help to keep them safe and warm. Some squirrels
make their nests inside tree trunks. Others build a
nest between the forked branches of a tree. This
type of nest is called a drey.

Red coats

The red squirrel's coat
can be red, brown, or
black. This squirrel has
tall, pointy ears.

Baby squirrels are
born blind, with very
little fur. After around
seven weeks, their
eyes are open and
their fur has grown.

The nest is lined
with moss, leaves,
feathers, fur and
grass to make
it cosy.

Squirrels are most active during daylight. They rarely leave their nests at night.

The mother squirrel wraps her tail around her babies like a blanket to keep them warm.

Rabbit warren

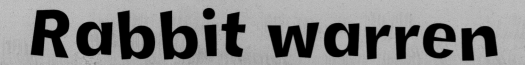

Rabbits use their strong legs and claws to dig an underground home. Their home is called a warren and it is made up of lots of tunnels and nesting areas joined together. A female rabbit is called a doe, and a male is called a buck.

Baby rabbits are called kits. They are born in a nest inside the warren that is lined with hay, straw and fur.

Newborn rabbits are blind and helpless. Their mother feeds them on her milk once a day.

A rabbit can dive into a tunnel to escape from predators such as birds of prey, foxes, weasels and cats.

Rabbits warn each other of danger by thumping their back feet on the ground.

Hare we go!
Hares look like rabbits, but are bigger and faster. They don't build warrens, but live in nests above ground.

Fun facts

Dormouse Sometimes, dormice make their nests in a hole in the ground, or in bird boxes fastened to trees.

Beaver These animals are excellent swimmers. Webbed back feet help beavers to move through the water. They steer with their large, flat tails.

Ant When the queen ant has mated, she flies back to her colony and goes underground. Her wings fall off, as she doesn't need to fly any more.

Polar bear To make a den, the mother bear digs a hole, then stamps on the snow to make a hard surface. She turns around and around to make the sides and top of the den hard.

Fox Look out for fox dens on steep slopes, under tree roots, or deep in the woods.

Weaver bird Some kinds of weaver birds build huge nests with separate areas to live in. They look like haystacks in a tree!

Wasp Wasps eat other insects, fruit, honey and meat from dead creatures.

Hermit crab Using its front claws, a hermit crab can block the entrance to its shell if it senses a predator nearby.

Squirrel Before winter starts, squirrels bury nuts and seeds so they have food to eat in cold weather.

Rabbit A female rabbit may have up to 12 babies at a time, and can reproduce several times a year.